YA 0...
Ande...
Wiki...

D0576493

DATE DUE

GAYLORD		PRINTED IN U.S.A.

WIKIPEDIA

ABDO
Publishing Company

TECHNOLOGY
PIONEERS

WIKIPEDIA

THE COMPANY AND ITS FOUNDERS

by Jennifer Joline Anderson

Content Consultant:
Joseph M. Reagle Jr.
Fellow, Berkman Center for Internet and Society
Harvard University

CREDITS

Published by ABDO Publishing Company, 8000 West 78th Street, Edina, Minnesota 55439. Copyright © 2011 by Abdo Consulting Group, Inc. International copyrights reserved in all countries. No part of this book may be reproduced in any form without written permission from the publisher. The Essential Library™ is a trademark and logo of ABDO Publishing Company.

Printed in the United States of America, North Mankato, Minnesota
112010
012011

 THIS BOOK CONTAINS AT LEAST 10% RECYCLED MATERIALS.

Editor: Mari Kesselring
Copy Editor: David Johnstone
Interior Design and Production: Craig Hinton
Cover Design: Emily Love

Library of Congress Cataloging-in-Publication Data
Anderson, Jennifer Joline.
  Wikipedia : the company and its founders / by Jennifer Joline Anderson.
      p. cm. — (Technology pioneers)
  Includes bibliographical references and index.
  ISBN 978-1-61714-812-5
  1. Wikipedia—Juvenile literature. 2. Electronic encyclopedias—Juvenile literature. 3. Wikis (Computer science)—Juvenile literature. 4. User-generated content—Juvenile literature. I. Title.
  AE100.A64 2011
  030—dc22
                                          2010037886

TABLE OF CONTENTS

Chapter 1   A New Kind of Encyclopedia   6

Chapter 2   Growing Up Curious   14

Chapter 3   The Internet Explosion   24

Chapter 4   The Nupedia Concept   34

Chapter 5   Making a Wiki   42

Chapter 6   Wikipedia Takes Off   50

Chapter 7   Going International   60

Chapter 8   Trolls, Vandals, and Edit Wars   70

Chapter 9   Controversy   80

Chapter 10   New Ventures   88

Timeline   96

Essential Facts   100

Glossary   102

Additional Resources   104

Source Notes   106

Index   110

About the Author   112

Jimmy Wales and Larry Sanger would team up to create a new kind of encyclopedia.

A NEW KIND OF ENCYCLOPEDIA

I t was the year 2000, the beginning of a new century and a new millennium. In San Diego, California, Jimmy Wales and Larry Sanger were working on a new kind of encyclopedia. They called it Nupedia.

Traditionally, the term *encyclopedia* had meant a series of printed volumes, assembled by professional editors, which provided information on topics from A to Z. Well-established and respected encyclopedias such as *World Book* and *Encyclopædia Britannica* were part of every reference library.

But Nupedia would be different. The first encyclopedia available only in electronic form; it would be free to anyone with an Internet connection. It would be created entirely by volunteer writers and editors. Nupedia would not belong to one company or individual, but would be freely available for the public to copy and reuse. And, as an electronic-only reference, there would be no limit to how big it could grow. Nupedia, its founders envisioned, would revolutionize encyclopedias.

Today, Wikipedia is the largest and most popular encyclopedia in the world. It contains more than 3 million articles in English, with more being added every day. Wikipedia has 272 world language versions—from German, Spanish, and Chinese to Urdu, Cherokee, and Kikuyu. The reason for Wikipedia's rapid growth is that anyone visiting the site can write or edit articles. As of June 2010, more than 12 million people had contributed to the English Wikipedia.

THE FIRST ENCYCLOPEDIAS

The word *encyclopedia* comes from two Greek words. The first is *enkyklios*, meaning "circular" or "rounded," and the second is *paideia*, meaning "education." Encyclopedias are collections of articles that provide a well-rounded education on many different topics. The first encyclopedias were created in Roman times. Perhaps the only ancient encyclopedia surviving today is *Naturalis Historia*, written by Roman philosopher Pliny the Elder. Published nearly 2,000 years ago, *Naturalis Historia* covers a wide variety of topics, including art, technology, mathematics, medicine, and nature. Although filled with myths and inaccuracies, the encyclopedia is interesting for what it reveals about the ancient world.

One of the largest encyclopedias in history was the Yongle encyclopedia, created in the thirteenth century in China under the emperor Yongle. It consisted of 11,095 volumes, all written by hand on scrolls.

The first alphabetical encyclopedias, which look the most like the encyclopedias of today, were created in the eighteenth century in Europe. They were printed on a printing press. The *Encyclopædia Britannica*, first published in Scotland between 1768 and 1771, is still in print more than 200 years later.

JIMMY WALES AND LARRY SANGER

Jimmy Wales, a 34-year-old Internet entrepreneur living in San Diego, had the idea for the Nupedia project. Wales, known to friends as "Jimbo," was a soft-spoken man with bright blue eyes and a closely cropped beard. He and partners Tim Shell and Michael Davis ran a Web site called Bomis, which people could use to find and share articles on a variety of topics. While never as popular as Yahoo! or Google, Bomis enjoyed a good business by selling space to advertisers. Wales used the money

from Bomis to start Nupedia. Eventually, he hoped
to profit by selling advertising space on Nupedia
as well.

Larry Sanger, age 31, was hired by Wales as
the editor in chief of Nupedia. A short, balding,
round-faced man with glasses, Sanger looked like
a stereotypical intellectual or computer geek. In
fact, he was both. He was just completing a PhD in
philosophy at Ohio State University and ran several
Web sites. This background made him a perfect
leader for Nupedia. Sanger's job was to recruit a team
of writers and editors and supervise them as they
created articles for the encyclopedia.

Before long, Sanger had a great team of
volunteers, many of them experts in their fields. But
they were making slow progress. By the end of 2000,
Nupedia had just over 20 entries. At that rate, it
would take years before it grew to the size of a real
encyclopedia. Something would have to change.

LET'S MAKE A WIKI

On January 2, 2001, Sanger met up with an old
friend, computer programmer Ben Kovitz, for dinner
at a taco shop. Among other topics, they discussed
the problems with Nupedia. Kovitz had an idea.

WHAT'S A WIKI?

The word Wikipedia is created by combining the word wiki with encyclopedia. A wiki is a Web site or group of sites that visitors can write and edit themselves. Ward Cunningham created the first wiki, WikiWikiWeb, in 1995. Cunningham believed that his new software would make editing the Web faster.

Wikipedia is just one of countless wikis available on the Internet today. Other popular user-created sites include WikiTravel (travel guides), WikiHow (how-to manuals), and WikiCars (a guide for cars and auto-related topics).

He had just heard of a Web site called WikiWikiWeb. The site was built in such a way that anyone reading it could make changes to it at any time, and the edits appeared instantly on the screen. It was easy to build and simple to use.

Sanger wondered whether WikiWikiWeb could be a good model for Nupedia. If many people could edit the encyclopedia at once, the process of writing articles would go a lot more quickly. Of course, if just anyone were allowed to make changes, there might be a lot of mistakes or even vandalism on the site. The idea was risky. Still, Sanger thought, it could work.

After receiving Wales's approval, Sanger sent out a message to his Nupedia team. The subject line was "Let's Make a Wiki." He explained the idea as follows:

Jimmy Wales had an idea for a free, electronic encyclopedia.

No, this is not an indecent proposal. It's an idea to add a little feature to Nupedia. . . . "Wiki," pronounced \wee'-kee\, derives from a Polynesian word, "wikiwiki," but what it means is a VERY open, VERY publicly-editable series of web pages. For example, I can start a page called EpistemicCircularity and write anything I want in it. Anyone else (yes, absolutely anyone else) can

"Imagine a world in which every single person on the planet is given free access to the sum of all human knowledge. That's what we're doing."[2]

—*Jimmy Wales*

come along and make absolutely any changes to it that he wants to.[1]

By January 15, 2001, Wikipedia was live on the Internet. By January 2002—just one year later—there were 20,000 articles. Wikipedia was well on its way to becoming what it is today: the largest and most popular encyclopedia in the world. +

Larry Sanger had the idea to make Nupedia into a wiki.

Jimmy Wales grew up near the Marshall Space Flight Center in Huntsville, Alabama.

GROWING UP CURIOUS

In 1968, Jimmy Donal Wales was not yet three years old when his mother, Doris Wales, bought the family's first set of encyclopedias from a door-to-door salesperson. Doris hoped the *World Book* encyclopedias would teach her son to love learning.

"I'm glad you got them, but don't you think he's a little bit young?" asked Jimmy's father, grocery store manager Jimmy Wales Sr.[1] But Jimmy learned to read at the age of four, and it was not long before he discovered the encyclopedias. The volumes were illustrated with colorful pictures and maps. "I spent many, many hours just pouring over the *World Book* encyclopedia," he remembered.[2]

However, there was one small problem with the encyclopedias. They could not keep up with the rapid changes that were happening in the world. New discoveries, especially in modern technology, made the books outdated quickly. To solve this problem, the publishers sent out stickers with updated information to be added to the encyclopedia. Each year, Jimmy and his mother would place the stickers in the books, learning new facts as they went along. Jimmy could never have imagined that one day he would make a new type of encyclopedia—one with millions of entries, all able to be updated instantly.

"[My parents] felt that education was important; it was always a passion in my household . . . the very traditional approach to knowledge and learning and establishing that as a base for a good life."[3]
—*Jimmy Wales, describing his early education*

ROCKET CITY

When Jimmy Wales was growing up in Huntsville, Alabama, the town was becoming known as "Rocket City." Scientists at NASA's Marshall Space Flight Center in Huntsville were creating the first rockets ever made in the United States. In the summer of 1969, when Jimmy was a toddler, astronaut Neil Armstrong became the first person to walk on the moon. All eyes were on outer space, and as he grew up in Rocket City, Jimmy shared in the excitement of the times. He told a reporter in 2006, "One of the things I remember was hearing the tests of the rockets when I was a kid. It had a very interesting influence on me. Growing up in Huntsville during the height of the space program, and all [the] exciting things going on with that, kind of gave you an optimist view of the future, of technology and science."[4]

SCHOOL DAYS

Jimmy Wales was born on August 7, 1966, in Huntsville, Alabama. Huntsville was home to the National Aeronautics and Space Administration (NASA) Marshall Space Flight Center, where scientists were developing the first US rockets to orbit Earth. Jimmy and his three younger siblings, Dori, DeeAnna, and Johnny, attended elementary school at the House of Learning in Huntsville. It was a small private school run by Jimmy's mother, Doris, and his grandmother, Erma. The school was similar to a one-room schoolhouse, in which children in different grades learn together. There were only four students in Jimmy's grade. Because the school was so small, Jimmy and his schoolmates enjoyed the freedom to choose what and how they wanted to learn. Jimmy became a curious student and an avid reader.

In 1979, Jimmy graduated from the House of Learning and went on to Randolph School, a private college preparatory school. Randolph was expensive, but Jimmy's parents felt he would receive a better education there than at the public high schools in Huntsville. Unlike the public schools, Randolph offered computers, and Jimmy spent a lot of time in the computer lab. "Anybody you'd find would say I was a geek," he confessed to a reporter about his high school days.[5]

DISCOVERING THE INTERNET

In the 1970s and early 1980s, personal computers (PCs) were still new, and few families owned them. The World Wide Web did not yet exist as an easy way to go online, and only people at universities or in government had access to the

THE FIRST PERSONAL COMPUTERS

The earliest computers were huge machines, taking up entire rooms. They were too large and too expensive for people to buy or use at home. It was not until the late 1970s that personal computers, or PCs, became available. At first, they were sold as electronic kits for hobbyists to put together. Then, in 1977, the Commodore PET and the Apple II were introduced as the first fully assembled personal computers. The Apple II computer became very popular. By the 1980s, Apple computers could be found in many schools. People used personal computers for games, word processing, and organization. "Surfing the Web" was unknown until the 1990s, however.

Jimmy Wales used early personal computers.

Internet. Jimmy began using the Internet when he attended college in the late 1980s, playing fantasy-adventure games on his computer. These early, multi-player games had no pictures, only text. Still, the simple games introduced Jimmy to the possibilities of the Internet, a vast, open space for people all over the world to connect.

A GAME PLAN

After graduating from high school, Wales entered Auburn University in Auburn, Alabama. Although he would one day become famous as an Internet pioneer, Wales did not study computer science or information technology in college. Instead, his interests led him to finance, the study of how money is exchanged and invested. He graduated with a bachelor's degree in finance in 1989.

At age 20, Wales married Pam, whom he had met while working at a grocery store. Pam remembers Wales as being very confident and ambitious. She recalled:

> *He was so sure of himself. . . . [I remember] flipping through the* Robb Report *at the grocery store where we worked, and there was this castle in England, and he said, "Yeah, we're going to have that one day. I'm going to be a millionaire before I'm 40." And it's like he's had a game plan ever since.*[6]

At the time, Wales's plan was to make it big in the investment business. In 1991, Wales earned a master's degree in finance at the University of Alabama. He also studied for his PhD in finance at the

BIRTH OF THE INTERNET

In 1969, the US Department of Defense started ARPANET (Advanced Research Projects Agency Network), an early version of the Internet, by linking together computers at several US universities. The first person to use ARPANET was a scientist at the University of California, Los Angeles (UCLA). He tried to connect to Stanford Research Institute in Palo Alto, California, on October 29, 1969. As he typed the word *login*, the system crashed. Only the first two letters of his message, *lo*, traveled over the net.

Two years later, the first e-mail was sent over ARPANET. By 1973, files could be shared over the network using a set of communication rules called the File Transfer Protocol, or FTP. That same year, ARPANET expanded its network, connecting to computers in Norway and London. Meanwhile, researchers Vinton Cerf at Stanford and Robert Kahn at ARPANET were designing a new set of rules for different computer networks to communicate with one another. Their rules, or "protocol," were called TCP/IP.

As computer networks all over the world began communicating using TCP/IP, they formed one giant global network known as the Internet. However, the Internet was not widely used until the early 1990s, when the World Wide Web was invented as an easy way to find and share information online.

University of Alabama and Indiana University. Eventually he quit school, however, to take a job in Chicago, Illinois, as a futures and options trader.

A KID FROM ALASKA

While Jimmy Wales was growing up in Alabama, his future Wikipedia partner, Larry Sanger, was far away in Alaska. Lawrence Mark Sanger was born on July 16, 1968, in Bellevue, Washington, a suburb of Seattle. When he was seven years old, his family moved to Anchorage, Alaska, where his father, Gerry, a marine biologist, worked for the US Fish and Wildlife Service. Larry spent summers on his father's boat in Prince William Sound. He learned about humpback whales and other creatures of the sea.

Like Jimmy, Larry was a curious student who loved learning. He read widely and learned to play the violin. Also like Jimmy, Larry enjoyed adventure games. As a teenager, Larry played the fantasy role-playing game Dungeons and Dragons. Players sat around a table and rolled an eight-sided die to move forward in the game. As Larry learned more about computers, he created his own text-based adventure game on his PC, using an early programming language called BASIC.

PHILOSOPHICAL MINDS

Sanger's curious nature led him to ask many questions about the world. In high school, he became interested in philosophy—the study of basic ideas about such things as knowledge, truth, and beauty. After graduating from high school in 1986, Sanger moved to Portland, Oregon, to attend Reed College. There, he earned a bachelor's degree in philosophy. He later earned a master's degree and a PhD in philosophy from Ohio State University.

PHILOSOPHY

The word *philosophy* comes from the Greek words for "love of wisdom." Philosophers use logic and reason to examine age-old questions, such as "What is beauty?" and "What is the meaning of life?" The area of philosophy that Sanger studied is called epistemology, which is concerned with the nature and meaning of knowledge itself—what knowledge is and how people acquire it. Objectivism, the philosophy that Wales became interested in, stresses the importance of rational self-interest and individual rights. Objectivists believe that people are motivated more by their own self-interest than by the desire to help others. They believe that society works best when individuals are allowed to pursue their own happiness.

Wales, too, had an interest in philosophy. When he was approximately 20 years old, he discovered the books of Ayn Rand. Rand was a Russian-American philosopher who developed the philosophy of objectivism in novels such as *The Fountainhead* and *Atlas Shrugged*. Rand's philosophy stressed the importance of reason, logic, and individual rights. Her ideas interested Wales so much that, in 1989, he created an Internet discussion board where people could discuss philosophy. One of the people who joined in the discussion was Sanger. Although neither of them knew it yet, these two philosophical minds would come together to influence the way the world thinks. +

Larry Sanger grew up in Anchorage, Alaska.

Netscape: Welcome to Netscape

Reload | Images | Open | Print | Find | Stop

scape.com/

l? | Handbook | Net Search | Net Directory | Newsgroups

W E L C O M E   T O   N E T S C A P E

EXPLORING THE NET | COMPANY & PRODUCTS | NETSCAPE STORE | NEWS & REFERENCE | ASSISTANCE | COMMUNITY

+ NETSCAPE SERVER GALLERIA +

SECURE COURIER
Netscape announces the first open, cross-platform "digital envelope" protocol, to be supported by Intuit, MasterCard, and others.

WINDOWS 95 NAVIGATOR BETA
Download the latest beta release of Netscape Navigator, specially tuned to take advantage of Win 95 interface enhancements and features.

SERVERMANIA
Test drive a fully loaded Netscape Commerce or Communications Server for 60 days and win the race for business server solutions. Now **free** for educational and charitable nonprofit institutions.

Early Internet browser Netscape Navigator launched in 1995.

THE INTERNET EXPLOSION

In the mid-1980s, the Internet existed but was still accessible only to people working in government or at schools and universities. Most people had no idea what it was. But in the early 1990s, two events created an Internet explosion.

First, the US government opened up the Internet for commercial use. For the first time, there could be advertising online—businesses could use the Internet to make money. The Internet was changing from a tool used by scientists and engineers into a global marketplace. Secondly, the World Wide Web was invented as an easy way to create, display, and link to information on the Internet.

Before the Web, using the Internet was a complicated process that required knowing how to use a series of commands. But with the Web's system of pointing and clicking, anyone with access to a computer could get online. The technology of the Web also made it easy to create Web pages using a language called Hypertext Markup Language (HTML).

Thousands of new Web sites were created, and thousands of users were going online every day. In 1993, the Web grew by an astonishing 341,000 percent, and it continued to grow through the rest of the decade. The Internet was becoming known as the "information superhighway," and

"Nobody who wasn't a high-energy physicist had even heard of the World Wide Web when I became President [in January 1993]. And now even my cat, Socks, has his own page."[1]
—President Bill Clinton, 1996

everyone wanted to get on. New phrases such as "surfing the Internet" became a part of everyday speech. The world had entered a new information age.

THE INTERNET AND THE WORLD WIDE WEB

Many people think the Internet and the Web are the same thing, but that is not quite true. The Internet is a worldwide network of computers, all able to communicate using a specific set of rules, or protocols, most importantly TCP/IP. The World Wide Web is just one part of the Internet. It is a collection of sites, pages, and files, all connected by hyperlinks. Users click on these highlighted words or icons to navigate from one part of the Web to another.

Invented by British computer scientist Sir Tim Berners-Lee in 1989 and introduced in 1990, the World Wide Web made navigating the Internet easier and faster. Users only have to open a Web browser, such as Internet Explorer or Mozilla Firefox, and type in the URL, or address, of the page they want to reach. The browser uses a set of rules called hypertext transfer protocol, or HTTP, to communicate with the Web server and bring up the desired page.

Surfing the World Wide Web is just one way of using the Internet. Other ways include sending e-mails and downloading files from an FTP site.

AN INTERNET ENTREPRENEUR

In 1996, Jimmy Wales was living in Chicago and working as a financial trader. His job was a challenge, as Wales found that the theories he had learned in school did not always work in the market. But Wales was a quick learner and made money in his trades. By night, Wales developed a hobby as a computer programmer. He kept up with online discussion groups and Internet mailing lists. With the growth of the Internet and the World Wide Web, Wales saw an opportunity to start a new business.

Wales and his partners Tim Shell and Michael Davis created a search site called Bomis. People used the site to find and share information on their favorite topics. The site made money by selling advertising space. But Wales dreamed of something even bigger. The World Wide Web was quickly making vast amounts of human knowledge available to people everywhere in the world. What if he could create a Web site that had information on every topic imaginable—a free electronic encyclopedia?

Wales's new idea presented several problems. Making an encyclopedia meant that he would need writers to create the entries and editors to edit them. Wales could not do it all himself, but he did not have enough money to pay a team of professional writers and editors. For his answer, Wales looked to the free software movement.

THE FREE SOFTWARE MOVEMENT

Since the 1970s, skilled computer programmers, or "hackers," had been working as a cooperative community. They would experiment with existing

Richard Stallman was responsible for the free software movement.

software, making changes that they shared with other users. In this way, the software continually improved yet remained free for everyone to use. In the 1980s, software developers began to copyright the software and make others pay to use it. This made the hackers angry. It meant they could not freely share and improve software. One of them, Richard Stallman, decided to fight back.

Stallman, a programmer at the prestigious Massachusetts Institute of Technology (MIT), came up with GNU, a project that developed software, that he put under what he called copyleft. Copyleft meant that under copyright law all modified versions of a software had the same rights as the original software. Unlike copyrights that restricted use of something, software under GNU Public License (GPL) had to be shared and could be modified by any user. GNU kicked off a free software movement. Finnish programmer Linus Torvalds adapted some of GNU's utilities to develop a free operating system called Linux. Over time, the hacker community shared their ideas, helping Torvalds develop Linux into a high-quality operating system that competes with Microsoft and other industry giants.

> "I consider that the golden rule requires that if I like a program I must share it with other people who like it."[2]
> —*Richard Stallman*

Wales decided his encyclopedia could be like GNU and Linux. It would be freely available on the Internet. It would be developed with the input of expert user-volunteers, not by a paid team. In what may have been a nod to Stallman's GNU, Wales named his project Nupedia.

FINDING AN EDITOR IN CHIEF

In 1997, Wales, now divorced from his first wife, remarried. By the following year, he had made enough money to quit his job in Chicago. He and his new wife, Christine, moved to San Diego, along with Wales's business partner Tim Shell. In California, Wales would concentrate full-time on Bomis and the Nupedia project.

Wales had a plan for Nupedia, but he still needed someone to lead his project. At this stage, Wales did not yet envision his encyclopedia as a wiki. Unlike the Wikipedia of today, Nupedia would be developed with the careful oversight of an editor in chief. The content would not be written by random users visiting the site, but by a team of qualified writers and expert editors. So, to begin the process, Wales needed to find his editor in chief.

Meanwhile, Larry Sanger was at Ohio State University, working on his PhD in epistemology. He was also busy with his own project on the Internet. As the year 2000, also referred to as Y2K, approached, the world of information technology was uneasy. Computer systems were not set up to read dates in the 2000s. Experts feared that when the year changed, computers all over the world would crash. They were racing against time to fix the problem before the new millennium began. To help people sift through all the stories about Y2K, Sanger and a friend created a Web site called Sanger's Review of Y2K News Reports.

Fortunately, New Year's Day 2000 came and went without any major problems. The world breathed a sigh of relief. And Sanger was soon looking for a new job. He sent out an e-mail to some of his online friends, proposing an idea for a new Web site.

One of those who received the e-mail was Jimmy Wales. Wales and Sanger had enjoyed debating on Wales's Internet philosophy discussion board and had even met in person a few times. Wales wanted someone with a philosophical mind to serve as the editor in chief of Nupedia. He thought Sanger was just the right

THE Y2K SCARE

In 1999, professionals who worked in information technology were facing a computer emergency. Many computer systems were set up to represent years in two digits, not four. Experts predicted that when the new year 2000, or Y2K, arrived, computers would misread the date '00 as 1900, causing systems to crash. Banks, government agencies, and other companies and institutions might lose all their information, throwing the world into chaos. In the worst case, people were afraid their bank accounts would be wiped clean, stores would be looted, and riots would break out in the streets. However, the Y2K bug was fixed before it was too late, and the New Year came without disaster.

candidate for the job. Wales wrote back, offering Sanger the chance to work for him.

Sanger was excited about the Nupedia project. "I thought I was very lucky to have a job like that land in my lap," he recalled.[3] In February 2000, he packed up his belongings and drove across the country to California, where he would start work on the revolutionary new encyclopedia. +

In the late 1990s, many computer companies prepared for Y2K.

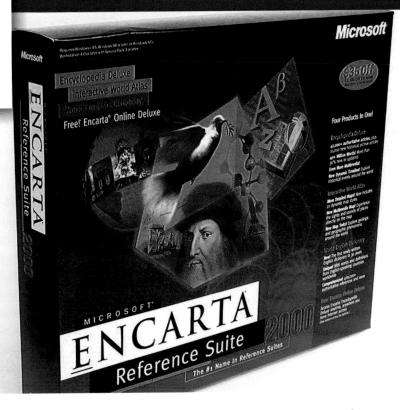

Encarta Reference Suite 2000 could be downloaded onto a computer and updated using the Internet.

THE NUPEDIA CONCEPT

S anger arrived in San Diego in February 2000, ready to begin work on Nupedia. By that time, a few encyclopedias were already available on the Internet, including *Encyclopædia Britannica* and Microsoft's *Encarta*. But Nupedia would differ from other encyclopedias in several important ways. Besides being completely free to read, the content of Nupedia would be available for anyone to copy and reuse, in the tradition of Richard Stallman's copyleft. Because of this, Wales saw the project as a radical philosophical mission. Nupedia's team of volunteer editors, writers, and reviewers would be creating a body of writing to be shared freely with the world.

"[O]ther people had had the idea [of an open source encyclopedia]; but it was Jimmy's fantastic foresight actually to invest in it. For this the world owes him a considerable debt."[2]

—*Larry Sanger*

Unlike other encyclopedias at the time, Nupedia would be developed specifically for the Internet and not for print. Therefore, there was no limit to how big it could grow. "Our goal is to create the largest encyclopedia the world has ever seen," wrote Sanger in 2000. "This will no doubt require years of work, but we are committed to that scale of endeavor."[1]

THE NUPEDIANS

Wales wanted Nupedia to be open for volunteers to develop. Now it was Sanger's job to figure out how to make this plan work. If the articles could be written by anyone, Sanger reasoned there needed to be expert editors assigning the articles and reviewing the material to make sure it was good enough to publish. He recalls in his memoir, "I maintained from the start that something really could not be a credible *encyclopedia* without oversight by experts."[3]

Sanger spent many hours recruiting editors, reviewers, and writers for Nupedia by e-mailing and posting to mailing lists. Prospective editors were asked to send in their résumés or curriculum vitae. Peer reviewers, too, were expected to be PhDs or to possess the equivalent publishing, teaching, or professional experience. Writers were not held to such a high standard.

NEUTRAL POINT OF VIEW

One of the first things Wales and Sanger agreed on was that Nupedia should have a neutral point of view. Being neutral meant that writers could not include opinion statements such as "The Beatles were the greatest band in history." They could, however, refer to opinions from reputable sources; for instance, "According to *Rolling Stone* magazine, the Beatles were the greatest band ever." When writing about controversial topics, writers were asked to represent arguments on all sides of the debate without stating which side they felt was right or wrong.

Neutral point of view, or NPOV, remains one of the fundamental principles of Wikipedia. Statements that show a bias, or clear opinion of the author, are quickly deleted in Wikipedia articles.

However, they were encouraged to post a member profile detailing their educational and professional qualifications.

The Nupedians were not paid for their work. The only compensation offered was a Nupedia coffee cup or T-shirt. But, as Sanger reminded his volunteers, they would be part of a very high-profile project that would have lasting value. He wrote:

> *We think there is . . . a clear incentive for experts to become involved, particularly as editors, writers, and peer reviewers. They will receive proper credit for their contributions on Nupedia, which will (in time) become one of the most important encyclopedias by virtue of its size, peer review mechanisms, editorial policies, and other features.[4]*

One year after the project was launched, 2,000 Nupedians were signed up to work on the encyclopedia.

A RIGOROUS PROCESS

Sanger outlined seven steps in the process of creating an article.

Step 1: The article was assigned to a writer by one of the "area editors."

Step 2: A lead reviewer was selected.

THE FIRST NUPEDIA ARTICLE

In September 2000, the first article made it through Nupedia's rigorous process and was posted online. The article was "Atonality," written by German music scholar Christoph Hust. The author was given credit for the article, along with the lead reviewer and copy editors. This is different from Wikipedia, in which authors and editors are not credited.

Step 3: The reviewer would read the article and offer suggestions for changes.

Step 4: The article was made available to a group of reviewers that made further suggestions.

Step 5: The article went to a lead copy editor, who corrected errors in grammar, spelling, and style.

Step 6: The article was edited by a group of copy editors.

Step 7: The article was approved by the area editor and made ready to go online.

The process was rather long and intimidating for some writers. Wales himself tried his hand at writing an article on economist Robert C. Merton. It was a topic he knew something about, having studied economic theories in school, but he found he could not finish the article. He later explained his writer's block:

I sat down to write the article, and I felt like I was back in graduate school, because they were going to give my paper to professors to review and

Nupedia made slow progress due to its rigorous editing process.

I was going to get comments and, you know, I might get a C grade or a B grade or something.[5]

For the first time, Wales wondered whether the Nupedia project would ever really get off the ground.

ENTER WIKIPEDIA

At the end of one year, Nupedia had produced only around 20 articles. The process was long and complicated, and the software the Nupedians were using to communicate made it difficult, too.

"[W]hat we didn't understand at that time is how to build a community and how to empower a community to do good work. So we had a lot of people really interested in the project because the vision of a free encyclopedia in every language was quite appealing to lots of really smart people. But . . . it was a very traditionally designed review process. There were seven stages and you had to submit your article and then it was reviewed by professors. And it was really not much fun."[6]

—*Jimmy Wales in 2005, explaining why the Nupedia project failed*

Wales had sunk $250,000 of Bomis's money into the project, and his investment seemed to be going nowhere fast.

So, when Sanger heard about wiki software in January 2001, he saw it as a way to save Nupedia. A wiki—a user-written Web site—would be a fast way to get the encyclopedia articles written. Called Wikipedia, the wiki site was originally intended to be just one part of Nupedia. Articles would be written by the Internet community on Wikipedia. They then would be carefully reviewed, polished, and added to Nupedia in their final form. But as it turned out, Wikipedia grew more quickly than anyone could have imagined. +

article	discussion	edit thi

History of London

From Wikipedia, the free encyclopedia

(Redirected from London History)

This

London, the capital of the United Kir
cultural capitals of the world. It has

Contents [hide]

On Wikipedia, articles would be written by the Internet community.

WIKIPEDIA

English
The Free Encyclopedia
3 102 000+ articles

日本語
フリー百科事典
633 000+ 記事

Deutsch
Die freie Enzyklopädie
983 000+ Artikel

Español
La enciclopedia libre
532 000+ artículos

Français
L'encyclopédie libre
877 000+ articles

Polski
Wolna encyklopedia
652 000+ haseł

Italiano
L'enciclopedia libera
628 000+ voci

Русский
Свободная энциклопедия
459 000+ статей

Português
A enciclopédia livre
522 000+ artigos

Nederlands
De vrije encyclopedie
572 000+ artikelen

search · suchen · rechercher · szukaj · 検索 · ricerca · zoeken · buscar · busca · поиск · sök · 搜索 · søk · haku · cerca · пошук · keresés · hledání · ara · căutare · serĉu · 찾기 · søg · suk · cari · hľadať · بحث · tìm kiếm · претрага

Wikipedia officially launched on January 15, 2001.

MAKING A WIKI

"**W**ikipedia is up!" Sanger wrote in an e-mail to the Nupedians on January 15, 2001. "Humor me. Go there and add a little article."[1] Sanger was not at all sure how the Nupedians would respond to the new wiki project.

As it turned out, most rejected the idea, finding it too informal and unstructured. They doubted that a good encyclopedia could be created using the wiki method, in which anyone and everyone was invited to write. Faced with a philosophical divide, Wales and Sanger decided to keep the two encyclopedia projects—Nupedia and Wikipedia—separate for the time being. Wikipedia was set up at its own domain, Wikipedia.com.

Bit by bit, quite a few Nupedians did get on board with the Wikipedia project, and new writers came over from other Web sites. By the end of January, Wikipedia boasted more than 600 articles. The concept was taking off more quickly than Wales and Sanger had imagined.

One of the reasons why Wikipedia caught on was that it was so easy to contribute to. Unlike Nupedia, there was no need for writers or editors to show credentials. They could even make changes anonymously, without creating an account or having a member ID.

"[Some Nupedians] evidently thought that a wiki *could* not resemble an encyclopedia at all, that it would be too informal and unstructured. . . . They of course were perfectly reasonable to doubt that it would turn into the fantastic source of content that it did. Who could reasonably guess that it would work? But it did work, and now the world knows better."[2]
—*Larry Sanger on the Nupedians who rejected Wikipedia*

THE WIKI SYSTEM

Wikipedia was built on wiki software called UseMod Wiki, developed by Clifford Adams. Later, German programmer and Wikipedia volunteer Magnus Manske made further changes to the software to create MediaWiki. UseMod Wiki and MediaWiki were both derived from Ward Cunningham's original WikiWikiWeb software. The basic idea behind the wiki software was that it allowed anyone to easily make changes to the site by clicking on the *edit* links on a page.

MediaWiki software also tracked all changes made to the article, making it easy for other users to see what was modified. If anyone were to make a bad change, it could be undone quickly. All earlier versions of the article were also saved so that if a vandal were to delete an article, it could be restored quickly.

IGNORE ALL RULES AND BE BOLD

Wikipedia had few rules and guidelines in the beginning. In fact, one of the first "rules" Sanger established for Wikipedia was "Ignore all rules," or IAR. It read, "If rules make you nervous and depressed, and not desirous of participating in the wiki, then ignore them entirely and go about your business."[3]

In order to help the wiki grow more and improve rapidly, Sanger encouraged Wikipedians to "Be bold" in editing and writing, and not to worry too much about making mistakes. After all, the wiki software made it easy to fix or undo errors. "Be bold in updating pages" remains one of the unofficial editing guidelines of Wikipedia.

Although it was important for users to ignore all rules and be bold sometimes, Wikipedia could not function without at least some rules. The three most important policies, as defined by Sanger, were neutral point of view (NPOV), verifiability (V), and no original research (NOR). These policies are still in effect.

EDITING WIKIPEDIA

To edit a Wikipedia article, users click on a link marked "edit." This brings them to an edit page where they can fix a mistake or add to the text using WikiMarkup language. For instance, to make a word appear in boldface, the user types three single quotation marks before and after the word. To make a word appear in italics, the user types two single quotes before and after the word.

To create a link in an article to another Wikipedia page, the user types two brackets before and after the word or phrase. For instance, typing [[Abraham Lincoln]] creates a clickable link to the Wikipedia article about Lincoln. If no such article exists, MediaWiki will automatically create a new article page. Writers are then welcome to start a brand-new article on that page.

Before saving any changes on the edit page, the user should briefly describe why the change was made. The MediaWiki software allows other users to review changes made to articles. If a bad change is made, another user can undo the change. If a new article does not meet the standards of Wikipedia, a site administrator can delete it.

Neutral point of view was borrowed from the Nupedia project. It simply means that articles cannot be written in support of any particular point of view or assert opinions on controversial topics. *Verifiability* means that a writer must cite reliable sources to back up any facts or opinions. The sources are presented as footnotes at the end of the article. *No original research* means that writers cannot present their own theories or ideas—everything on Wikipedia must be taken from reliable, published sources. For instance, a scientist cannot present a new theory about gravity on Wikipedia unless he or she has already published an article about it in a recognized scientific journal.

In the early months of Wikipedia, many users wrote articles that Sanger felt did not belong in an encyclopedia. Some of them were too much like dictionary entries—much too short. Some were about topics that were not notable or famous, such as a person's unknown garage band or pet cat. Others were written like advertisements or contained the writer's original ideas on a subject. To help guide writers in creating good encyclopedia entries, Sanger wrote a page called "What Wikipedia Is Not." Among other things, he explained that Wikipedia is not a dictionary, not a publisher of original thought, not a soapbox or means of promotion, not a blog or social networking site, not a textbook made to teach people, and not a means for making predictions about the future.

The Wikipedia community soon became familiar with what made a good article. With the wiki format, Sanger no longer had to act as the leader. Wikipedians themselves identified poor articles and either corrected them over time or voted to have them deleted. It became a truly collaborative effort.

BUILDING A COMMUNITY

"The design of Wikipedia," Wales said, "is the design of community."[4] As the community grew throughout 2001, changes were made to help writers and editors communicate better. A separate Discussion page was created for each article so that editors could comment on articles and debate ways to improve them. A Village Pump page was set up for discussion about Wikipedia in general. A page called Articles for Deletion

NOT SO ANONYMOUS

Visitors to Wikipedia can make changes without creating a username or logging in. However, this does not make them completely anonymous. Every computer connected to the Internet has an IP (Internet Protocol) address that may indicate what service provider is being used and approximately where the computer is located. When a user does not log in, Wikipedia records the user's IP address instead. If the user vandalizes the site, his or her IP address can be blocked.

allowed people to discuss articles being considered
for removal. Users got to know one another by
creating their own pages with personal details about
themselves.

Sanger was very pleased with the way the
community of users had developed. The wiki project
could easily have been taken over by pranksters
and vandals filling up the pages with nonsense. But
somehow, that did not happen. In 2001, Sanger
explained how a strong democratic community had
gathered to make Wikipedia work:

> *We're constantly cleaning up after each other and
> new people. In the process, a camaraderie—a
> politeness and congeniality not found on many
> online discussion forums—has developed. We've
> got to respect each other, because we are each
> other's editors, and we all have more or less the
> same goal: to create a huge, high-quality free
> encyclopedia.*[5] +

Wales appreciated the community that Wikipedia inspired.

Wikipedia became popular very quickly.

WIKIPEDIA TAKES OFF

Wikipedia grew, and kept on growing, at an amazing rate. By July 8, 2001, there were 6,000 articles. By August 7, there were 8,000. There were 11,200 by September 9 and 13,000 by October 4. One year after the project began, in January 2002, there were 20,000 articles on Wikipedia. Wales described the phenomenon using an unusual metaphor:

> *In French Wikipedia they came up with a fantastic phrase; they call it the piranha effect. You start with a little tiny article and it's not quite good enough so people are picking at it in sort of a feeding frenzy and articles grow.*[1]

Piranhas are a kind of fish with sharp teeth and an appetite for meat. When one starts to feed, all the rest join the feeding out of instinct. In much the same way, Wikipedians swarm together to "attack" topics until they are picked clean.

WHY CONTRIBUTE?

In interviews with the press and in his memoir about the project, Sanger attempted to explain the unique spirit of collaboration that created Wikipedia. He pointed out that Wikipedians were inspired by the site's open-content license. Wikipedia used GNU Free Documentation License (GFDL). GFDL was similar to GPL except that it related to text instead of software. The license guaranteed that no individual could claim ownership of a work and any modifications had to be shared. Sanger added:

We promised contributors that their work would always remain free for others to read. This, as is well known, motivates people to work for the good of the world—and for the many people who would like to teach the whole world, that's a pretty strong motivation.[2]

Another important reason why people wanted to contribute, Sanger felt, was because Wikipedia was very accessible. The wiki software was easy to learn and the community was welcoming. "There was no sense that someone would be turned away for not being bright enough, or not being a good enough writer, or whatever," Sanger explained.[3]

For some contributors, Wikipedia became an obsession. Derek Ramsey, also known as Ram-Man, logged nearly 200,000 edits on Wikipedia and contributed tens of thousands of articles with the help of a software robot, which he named "Rambot." Because of Ramsey, articles exist on Wikipedia about every town and city in the United States. Ramsey has also uploaded more than 1,000 of his own photographs to illustrate Wikipedia articles.

Another famous Wikipedian, Seth Ilys, started creating maps for each town and county of his home state of North Carolina in 2004. Soon, he was addicted, spending hours of his time each day on his mission to create a map for every city and county in the nation.

But he was not the only one. Others saw what Ilys was doing and joined his project. The Wikipedian piranhas converged, taking bite by bite out of the massive undertaking.

A COMMUNITY

Wikipedia was able to grow so quickly because of the community it created. Many of the people attracted to the project were already familiar with the idea of communicating on the Internet's bulletin boards, forums, and other types of Web sites.

RAM-MAN AND THE RAMBOT

Derek Ramsey, also know as Ram-Man, discovered Wikipedia in 2002. He had just earned his computer science degree from Rochester Institute of Technology and had not yet found a job, so he had free time.

Ramsey was interested in geography, and he noticed that Wikipedia lacked information about many cities and towns in the United States. He thought of a way to get the information he needed: from the US census. Every ten years, the US government conducts a census to collect information about the population and the economy. With data from the 2000 census freely available on the Internet, Ramsey set out to create an article for every US city and county.

Ramsey spent many hours copying and pasting the information into Wikipedia articles. But after finishing 3,000 articles, he realized he needed a quicker way. Ramsey created a software program, known as a robot or bot, which would prepare the articles for him and add them to Wikipedia. In just one week, from October 19, 2002, through October 25, 2002, the "Rambot" had added an astonishing 33,832 articles—more than doubling the size of Wikipedia and making Ram-Man a legend. Never again has Wikipedia grown so quickly.

With the principle of neutrality, the community was able to work together without too much conflict. And since the content was open—not owned by any single author—collaboration was possible. People could edit anyone else's work. Wales explained:

> One of the big misconceptions about Wikipedia—people imagine that it's something like one million people each adding one sentence each and somehow miraculously it becomes something useful. But in fact what actually makes it work is the community. There's a really strong community of people behind the site and they are in constant communication by email and IRC chat rooms and things like this. And so they are monitoring every change that goes to the site, there are people who are looking at it and vetting it and trying to see if it's good or not.[4]

Guided by the principles of neutrality and collaboration, the community was able to create in a short time what no individual or smaller team could have accomplished.

INCLUSIONISTS AND EXCLUSIONISTS

As the encyclopedia grew, Wikipedians continued to debate about which articles should be included and which should be excluded. The inclusionists argued that since Wikipedia was not a paper encyclopedia, any and all topics should be included. Exclusionists argued that too many articles on unimportant topics would make the encyclopedia messy and hard to take seriously.

The first question to ask when assessing an article subject, the Wikipedians decided, was "Is it notable?" In order to be notable, the subject must have received coverage in reliable sources, such as respected books, newspapers, and magazines either online or in print. Articles that did not meet the notability requirement could be nominated for removal on the Articles for Deletion page (originally Votes for Deletion). There, they were discussed until a consensus was reached about their notability.

Occasionally, however, articles had to be deleted right away with no discussion. These were articles that violated someone's privacy, plagiarized someone

"Wikipedia has the potential to be the greatest effort in collaborative knowledge gathering the world has ever known, and it may well be the greatest effort in voluntary collaboration of any kind."[5]
—*Marshall Poe, writing in The Atlantic*

JUST A STUB

Many of the articles in Wikipedia start out as mere stubs—that is, incomplete articles in need of expansion. Visitors to Wikipedia who are looking for a way to help grow the encyclopedia can start by looking for stubs. Users can browse stubs by category on Wikipedia and find stubs they can add to.

else's writing, or insulted someone. All such articles could lead to legal trouble for Wikipedia. Wales and Sanger could not personally respond to every such instance, so Wales chose some Wikipedia editors to be administrators, or "sysops" (system operators). These administrators had the power to delete articles, lock down pages that were being vandalized, or block problem users. Not surprisingly, some Wikipedians objected to the idea of administrators. A true wiki, they felt, should be a pure democracy. Wales understood their objections and emphasized that being a sysop was not a huge deal.

NUPEDIA LEFT BEHIND

In July 2001, Sanger started a new wiki called Chalkboard, which was intended for moving Wikipedia articles into Nupedia. However, the Chalkboard project never really caught on, and with all the work he was doing for Wikipedia, Sanger had little time left to help Nupedia grow. Eventually, Nupedia was abandoned altogether. Sanger regretted the loss. Although it had not grown quickly enough, he continued to feel that, with Nupedia's rigorous editing process, it was a more reliable resource than Wikipedia could hope to become. In a memoir written later about Nupedia and Wikipedia, Sanger reflected:

> *[Nupedia] could have been redesigned and adapted—it could have, as it were, 'learned from its mistakes' and from Wikipedia's successes. Thousands of people who had signed up and who wanted to contribute to the Nupedia system were left disappointed. I believe this was unfortunate and unnecessary; I always wanted Nupedia and Wikipedia working together to be not only the world's largest but also the world's most reliable encyclopedia.[6]*

Sanger was not the only one worried about the reliability of Wikipedia. Even as the online encyclopedia became wildly popular, it was criticized in the press as an unreliable resource. Most Wikipedians cared about the project and worked hard to fix errors, but some were careless, unreasonable, or even destructive. With no system in place for experts to review the articles, Sanger was becoming frustrated. He wondered whether anything could be done to fix the problem. +

Sanger was disappointed that Nupedia had to be abandoned.

Wales was passionate about bringing Wikipedia to other countries.

GOING INTERNATIONAL

Wikipedia started out as an English-language encyclopedia. However, from the very first months, articles began appearing in different languages, showing that the international community was involved and interested in Wikipedia. So, in March 2001, Wales created the first non-English Wikipedia for articles written in German, deutsche.wikipedia.com. Today, the German language version has more than 1 million articles, making it the second-largest edition after English Wikipedia.

Many more language versions, including French, Spanish, Catalan, Hebrew, Italian, and Japanese, followed soon after the German one. In September 2001, Wikipedia announced that it would be setting up sites for all the major languages. Wikipedia was going international.

CULTURAL DIFFERENCES

The foreign-language versions were more than just word-for-word translations of the English Wikipedia. Each one developed its own cultural flavor. For example, the Japanese entry for "dog" includes a picture of a Shiba Inu, a Japanese dog

WIKIPEDIA GETS BLOCKED

Wikipedia has become popular all over the world. However, it has not been so popular with some governments, which have blocked the site periodically. Wikipedia has been blocked multiple times in China, once for an entire year, from October 2005 to October 2006. The site has also been censored for short periods in Iran, Syria, Pakistan, Thailand, Tunisia, the United Kingdom, and Uzbekistan.

Governments typically block Wikipedia in order to censor information about politically controversial topics. Wikipedia is opposed to such censorship.

breed. The German entry shows a German shepherd, and the Swedish entry shows a Norwegian elkhound.

Some Wikipedians argued that because of cultural and spelling differences, English Wikipedia should be split into two versions: British English and American English. They pointed out that, for example, British speakers refer to potato chips as "crisps," and spell *flavor* as *flavour*. For that reason, an article such as "potato chips" could cause confusion. In the end, however, English Wikipedia was not split. Instead, the decision was made to use British spellings for British topics and American spellings for American topics.

REPRESENTING FOREIGN CHARACTERS

As Wikipedia grew to include Asian languages, a technical problem arose. The wiki software had been created to accommodate the Roman alphabet used in English and most other Western languages. However, it could not represent characters such as those found in Chinese, Japanese, Korean, and many other world languages. Chinese, in particular, posed a problem, as it uses many thousands of different characters.

One possible solution was to convert to a different language system, called Unicode. Unicode had been created in 1991, as the Internet was becoming more international. It could represent all possible symbols of all the world's languages. However, Wikipedia needed a Unicode system that would not take up much space. Some Unicode systems needed a lot of storage, which could make Wikipedia very slow.

Luckily, a suitable system existed. It was a Unicode encoding system called UTF-8, developed by software developer Ken Thompson and his friend Rob Pike in 1992. UTF-8 was designed to be space efficient and was compatible with the system already being used on Wikipedia. UTF-8 was adopted

HELP FOR CHINESE WIKIPEDIA

In 2004, a Chinese student with the username ZhengZhu solved a big problem with Chinese Wikipedia. Chinese speakers have two different versions of their written language. Simplified Chinese is used in mainland China, while the more complex traditional Chinese is used in Taiwan, Hong Kong, and other Chinese-speaking areas. For instance, the word China (zhōng guó) written in traditional Chinese is 中國. However, in simplified Chinese, it is 中国.

Wikipedia needed an easy way to convert one form of Chinese to another so that visitors to the site could choose which version they preferred. ZhengZhu, working entirely as a Wikipedia volunteer, developed a computer program that would do just that. ZhengZhu's innovative software also came in handy in converting other language versions, such as Serbian, which can be written in either the Roman alphabet or the Cyrillic (Russian) script.

Wikipedia was the first public project that needed to handle so many different languages in one program. It succeeded because of the input of smart people such as ZhengZhu, who were willing to work simply for the satisfaction of helping to share knowledge around the globe.

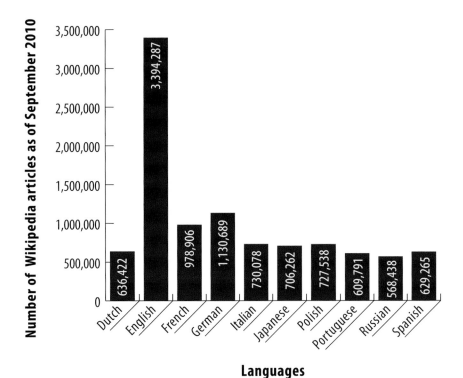

immediately, allowing languages such as Chinese, Japanese, and Korean to find homes on Wikipedia.

THE SPANISH FORK DISASTER

The Spanish Wikipedia was one of the earliest international versions. By February 2002, Wikipedian Edgar Enyedy reported that the site had reached its first 1,000 useful articles. But less than one week later, the buoyant mood changed completely.

Up until this time, Wales's company, Bomis, had provided the funding for Wikipedia. Now, Bomis was running out of money. Like many companies that had invested in the Internet boom, it was suffering losses as the market began to fall. Wales could no longer afford to pay Sanger a salary for his job as editor in chief, and Sanger was laid off. He continued working for Wikipedia as a volunteer while looking for another full-time job. Still, Sanger was hopeful that there might be a solution to Wikipedia's money problems. In a message to other Wikipedians on February 12, Sanger wrote, "Bomis might well start selling ads on Wikipedia . . . and revenue from those ads might make it possible for me to come back to my old job."[1]

It had always been Wales's idea to make money by selling ads on Wikipedia. But the idea did not sit well with the many unpaid volunteers who had made the new encyclopedia such a huge success. Enyedy was one of them. He fired off the following angry message:

> *Nobody is going to make even a simple buck placing ads on my work, which is clearly intended for [the] community. . . . Nobody is going to use my efforts to pay wages or maintain servers. And*

I'm not the only one who feels this way. I've left the project. . . . Good luck with your wikiPAIDia.[2]

On February 26, 2002, Enyedy created a new "fork," or copy, of Spanish Wikipedia, which he named Enciclopedia Libre. Much like a fork in the road, the "Spanish fork" marked a place where the Spanish-speaking Wikipedians and the rest of the project would go their separate ways. Enyedy took most of the Spanish-language Wikipedians with him to the new site. Spanish Wikipedia suffered from the loss. For more than a year, it lagged behind, with few volunteers left. However, in time, a new community formed, and Spanish Wikipedia resumed its steady growth.

DOT COM AND DOT ORG

Web site addresses that end in *.com* are used by for-profit businesses. Those ending in *.org* are used by nonprofit organizations. Wikipedia moved from *wikipedia.com* to *wikipedia.org* when it established itself as a nonprofit organization in 2003.

GOING NONPROFIT

The Spanish fork taught Wales a lesson. Volunteer writers and editors would not want to participate if they felt someone was profiting from their efforts. It was important for Wikipedia to stay a nonprofit. In June 2003, Wales created the nonprofit Wikimedia Foundation to run Wikipedia.

Donations to the foundation would provide the money to keep Wikipedia running and pay the salaries for its few full-time employees.

Making Wikipedia a nonprofit meant that Wales could not become rich by selling ad space on Wikipedia. In a 2007 interview, Wales confessed that making Wikipedia nonprofit was both the "dumbest and the smartest" thing he had ever done:

> *The dumbest because it's probably worth $3 billion—and I don't have $3 billion! It's also the smartest thing I did because it wouldn't have been anywhere near so successful had I not built it this way.*[3]

FUTURE GROWTH

Although Wikipedia had grown to include articles in approximately 272 languages as of 2010, many foreign-language Wikipedia versions are much smaller than others. For instance, 73 languages, including many used in African nations, have fewer than 1,000 articles. It is a good start for some languages, which might not have any type of encyclopedia in any form. However, an encyclopedia with fewer than 1,000 entries is not very useful. In order for these struggling foreign-language

"Our goal is, and always has been since I first dreamed up the idea of a free encyclopedia, a grandiose goal of an effort to generate the greatest encyclopedia on the planet, for free. My primary interest in doing this is ultimately in seeing it distributed at very low cost to every person on the planet, even in poverty-stricken countries with little or no access to the Internet or traditional forms of education. Knowledge is power. And we want to put the power of knowledge into the hands of every person in the world."[5]
—*Jimmy Wales, 2002*

Wikipedias to make a difference, they need volunteers to help them grow.

One major problem is that Internet access is limited in developing countries. It is difficult—and somewhat pointless—to build a wiki in places where few people can even get online. Still, in November 2009, Wales said that he hoped to grow Wikipedia in Africa and other parts of the developing world. "I think it's important for Wikipedia, but I also think it's important for the world," he commented. "We're going to start getting cultural influences from places that we know almost nothing about today."[4] +

A book titled *One-Volume Wikipedia Encyclopedia*, which includes 50,000 of the most-searched terms in the German language edition, was published in Germany.

Some Wikipedians called Jimmy Wales "Benevolent Dictator."

TROLLS, VANDALS, AND EDIT WARS

Wikipedians have affectionately referred to Wales as "Benevolent Dictator."[1] Sanger once joked that he was "Dictator for Life."[2] However, the two founders never exerted all-controlling power over the Wikipedia project.

Wikis are more like democratic systems—nobody is king.

As Wales and Sanger found out, Wikipedia's democratic-like system had benefits as well as drawbacks. Wikipedia's bottom-up structure—in which the people at the bottom had most of the power—allowed the site to grow very quickly. On the other hand, the lack of control led to chaos at times.

From the beginning, most Wikipedians were there to help make the encyclopedia better. However, as with any project, there were people who seemed to only cause destruction and disorder. They were known as trolls and vandals.

TROLLS

A troll is someone who hides behind the anonymity of the Internet, waiting to stir up conflict by posting controversial or inappropriate messages or by insulting other users. A troll often pretends to be sincere while drawing others into a pointless, never-ending argument. Trolls can cause a lot of problems on a site like Wikipedia.

"Any place where the general public is allowed to freely express their opinion without having any sort of prior approval from authority—it is dangerous. Free speech is dangerous. But it's also incredibly powerful and useful."[3]

—*Jimmy Wales*

The most effective way, typically, to confront problematic users who are perhaps trolls is to ignore them. But Wikipedia's format made it very difficult to do so. Their actions and messages could easily disrupt the progress of the encyclopedia.

One way in which users caused trouble on Wikipedia was by posting offensive articles and then pretending not to understand why the postings were being deleted. Another way was to enter into edit wars—they would repeatedly change text back after others edited it. They would also engage in flame wars—arguments that became nothing more than an exchange of insults. Sanger noticed that some of the site's expert editors were leaving the project because they were tired of working with

THE GDANSK/DANZIG EDIT WAR

One of the most famous edit wars on Wikipedia took place when users could not agree on the proper name for a city in northern Poland. Gdansk is the city's Polish name; however, since it was at one time a part of Germany, it is also known by the German name of Danzig. The war reached its height in October 2003, when two users went back and forth many times per day, one changing Gdansk to Danzig and the other reversing the change.

This led to a new rule on Wikipedia called the three revert rule (3RR). It holds that any user who reverts the same text more than three times in one day is banned from editing for the next 24 hours. The rule, backed by Wales, helped to prevent the worst edit wars.

But even with the new rule, the Gdansk/Danzig war was not settled for nearly two years, when a compromise was struck to refer to the city as Gdansk in some situations and Danzig in others.

problematic users who did not respect their expertise. The loss of highly educated Wikipedians, Sanger felt, was damaging the quality of the encyclopedia.

Before Sanger was laid off in 2002, he tried to address these issues on Wikipedia. Viewing himself as something of a leader on Wikipedia, he attempted to intervene when he saw troll-like behavior. But when he did so, other Wikipedians sometimes came to the troll's defense. Sanger was becoming increasingly frustrated. "Short of removing the problem contributors altogether—which we did only in the very worst cases—there was no easy solution," Sanger recalls. "Fires were spreading everywhere, and . . . I did not have quite enough allies to help me put them out."[4]

THE CUNCTATOR

Things really heated up in October 2001, when a user called "The Cunctator" started an edit war with Sanger, challenging Sanger's edits and deletions. The Cunctator was something of an anarchist, and he felt that Sanger was trying to claim too much power over Wikipedia. When Sanger tried to have the last word, The Cunctator kept on fighting. At last, Sanger wrote the following note to the Wikipedia community:

NO ANGRY MASTODONS

Wikipedians developed norms, or guidelines, for users to follow in order to avoid conflict. Some of the most important norms are explained below:

Assume good faith (AGF): Do not automatically assume the other person is mean-spirited. Assume they are acting in the best interest of Wikipedia.

Avoid personal remarks (APR): Avoid making comments directed at the person, such as "You're wrong." Instead, keep your focus on the issue, as in: "I believe the edit you made here is wrong."

No angry mastodons (NAM): There is no need to behave like a prehistoric beast. Keep the discussion civilized. If you feel angry, take a break. Do not respond until you are able to respond calmly.

I need to be granted fairly broad authority by the community . . . if I am going to do my job effectively. Until fairly recently, I was granted such authority by Wikipedians. I was . . . called to justify decisions I made, but not constantly and nearly always respectfully and helpfully. This place in the community . . . [made] me a leader. That's what I want, again. This is my job.[5]

The Cunctator responded by writing a sarcastic essay and posting it on Wikipedia. In the essay, he sharply criticized Sanger for being too much like a dictator. For Sanger, this was the last straw. With no respect for leadership in Wikipedia, he felt the trolls were winning.

SANGER LEAVES

In December 2001, Sanger went to Las Vegas, Nevada, to get married.

Sanger got married in Las Vegas in 2001.

It was a happy time in his life. Unfortunately, it was just a few weeks later that, because Bomis was failing and Wales could no longer afford to pay him, Sanger was laid off.

Sanger stayed on as a volunteer at Wikipedia for awhile, resigning permanently in March 2002. He left on good terms. Still, he wrote that he might have stayed longer as a volunteer had it not been for the "difficult people, trolls, and their enablers" who were creating a "poisonous political and social atmosphere" on Wikipedia.[6] Sanger wished the project the best of luck, but he had serious doubts about its future.

With Sanger gone, Wales was left as the sole leader of Wikipedia. His style was somewhat different from Sanger's. He was relatively hands-off, intervening in only the most difficult cases rather than becoming involved in day-to-day activities. He felt that the Wikipedia community could run itself without too much guidance from him. Because of his laid-back style, he was not as troubled by trolls. However, there was one problem Wales was often called on to confront—vandalism.

VANDALS AND SOCK PUPPETS

Vandals are the most obvious abusers in the Wikipedia world. They do such things as delete all the text in an article, write childish things in articles, or add offensive pictures. Wikipedians are constantly on the lookout for vandalism. The wiki software provides them with a way to check up on recently changed pages. If they see anything suspicious, they are able to fix it immediately. In addition, Wikipedia began using software bots that detect and fix many common acts of vandalism automatically. Most vandals give up after one or two attempts to cause trouble when they see that their pranks are quickly erased.

One solution to vandalism is to block the user's Internet address, either temporarily or permanently. However, Wales was reluctant to do this unless absolutely necessary. Some vandals worked from computers in schools or libraries. If Wikipedia were to block these vandals, the entire school or library system could be blocked as well.

Another solution for problem users—both trolls and vandals—was to ban the individual users. But this did not always work either, because the troll or vandal could create a new user account and pretend to be someone else. A fake user account, created for the purpose of trolling or vandalizing, became known as a sock puppet. The infamous Wikipedia vandal called "Willy on Wheels," for instance, created dozens of sock puppets in order to do damage. The puppets appeared to be new, innocent users, but Willy on Wheels controlled all of them.

As Wikipedia grew, Wales could no longer solve all the

WILLY ON WHEELS

Perhaps the worst Wikipedia vandal was Willy on Wheels. This vandal used a software bot to move pages all over Wikipedia, changing the titles of the articles to add "on Wheels!" For instance, the entry for Jimmy Wales became "Jimmy Wales on Wheels!" The damage created by Willy on Wheels took a long time to fix. Eventually, the Willy on Wheels vandal apologized for his behavior. He said that after Wikipedia helped him with an important school project, he realized the value the site had and would no longer vandalize it.

problems with trolls, vandals, and sock puppets. In 2001, he had named certain users as administrators. Later, in 2004, he created a new committee, called the Arbitration Committee, or ArbCom, to help resolve disputes. ArbCom worked together to confront problem users, banning or blocking them when necessary.

ArbCom was solving some of the core problems with Wikipedia's system that had bothered Sanger so much. But challenges remained for the online encyclopedia. +

Most users contributed to Wikipedia in a positive way, while others hid behind the anonymity of the Internet to wreak havoc.

John Seigenthaler was wrongfully linked to the Kennedy assassinations in a Wikipedia entry.

CONTROVERSY

In September 2004, Wikipedia reached 1 million articles in more than 100 languages. Around the world, it was quickly becoming a favorite source of information. Wikipedia was extremely up to date, with new articles and facts being added every hour. But as it became more popular, Wikipedia became more controversial. Teachers and professors complained that students were relying too much on the online encyclopedia instead of consulting more trustworthy resources. Several well-publicized incidents showed that it could be dangerous to trust what one read on Wikipedia.

In November 2004, the former editor in chief of *Encyclopædia Britannica,* Robert McHenry, wrote a lengthy critique of Wikipedia, called "The Faith-Based Encyclopedia." In the essay, he compared Wikipedia to a public restroom—it may look clean, but you never know who used it last. McHenry's words were harsh, but there was some truth to them. Traditional encyclopedias such as *Encyclopædia Britannica* and *World Book* contain entries written and edited by experts in their fields. For instance, the article on space-time in the thirteenth edition of *Encyclopædia Britannica* was written by none other than Albert Einstein. By contrast, there was no way of knowing who wrote or altered an article on Wikipedia. Even if the original writer were an expert, random people could come along later to make edits, introducing errors and bad writing.

Because of this hazard, people were asking—and continue to ask—one big question: How reliable is Wikipedia?

THE JOHN SEIGENTHALER HOAX

In September 2005, a startling hoax made news in the United States, starting a nationwide debate about Wikipedia's reliability. An anonymous user had created an article on Wikipedia about US journalist John Seigenthaler. In the article, the user falsely claimed that Seigenthaler had been a suspect in the assassinations of President John F. Kennedy and his brother Robert Kennedy in the 1960s.

In fact, the 78-year-old Seigenthaler did have a link to the Kennedys—he had been the assistant and friend of Robert Kennedy and a pallbearer at his funeral. Seigenthaler was hurt—and angry. A colleague helped Seigenthaler by removing the libelous text, and Wales deleted it from Wikipedia's history pages. The IP address was traced to a man named Brian Chase in Tennessee. Chase apologized to Seigenthaler, saying it was all "a joke that went

"I do not trust what I ingest on the Internet because I know how the digital sausage is made."[1]
—*Larry Sanger, criticizing Wikipedia and other Web sites as unreliable in 2009*

horribly, horribly wrong."[2] He had edited the article to trick a friend who knew the Seigenthaler family.

But by the time the hoax biography was discovered and corrected, it had already been on the site for four months. The false information had spread to other Internet sites. Seigenthaler wrote an article about the incident in *USA Today*, criticizing Wikipedia as a "flawed and irresponsible research tool."[3]

The prank led Wikipedia to change some of its policies. After the Seigenthaler incident, only editors with a user account could create new articles; it could no longer be done anonymously. Biographies of living people were also subject to more editorial control. Administrators now had the power to protect biography pages from being edited in a malicious or biased manner.

THE ESSJAY SCANDAL

In 2007, another scandal harmed Wikipedia's reputation. It involved a user named Essjay. Essjay claimed to be a tenured professor of religion at a private university. His user profile indicated that he had two PhDs that made him an expert in theology and the Catholic Church. Other Wikipedians respected

Essjay and regarded him as a trusted member of the community. In fact, he even became an administrator of Wikipedia with the authority to check user IPs. Essjay was profiled in a *New Yorker* magazine article, which held him up as an example of the quality of writers and editors at Wikipedia.

There was one problem: Essjay was not who he claimed to be. He was actually Ryan Jordan, a 24-year-old high school graduate from Kentucky. He did not hold a single college degree and had never taught anywhere. When the truth came out in 2007, Essjay said he had lied in order to protect himself from trolls on Wikipedia.

Wales's first reaction was that it did not matter who Essjay really was as long as he did good work. He

SNEAKY EDITING ON WIKIPEDIA

Because anyone can edit Wikipedia, it is not surprising that many have edited it to make themselves look better—including major companies and politicians. On November 17, 2005, 15 paragraphs were deleted from an article about the company Diebold. The deleted paragraphs contained criticism about the company's product, electronic voting machines. Wikipedians traced the anonymous editor's IP address and found that the changes had come from someone working for Diebold. The deleted paragraphs were put back in place immediately.

In 2006, several politicians' campaign workers were found to have edited articles to make their candidates look better, removing criticism and adding words of praise. At least one campaign manager actually added negative information about opponents. Their actions were revealed to the media to discourage others from trying the same tactic.

said, "To me, the important thing is getting it right. I don't care if they're a high school kid or a Harvard professor."[4] However, after learning more about Essjay's deception and how upsetting it had been for other Wikipedians, Wales changed his mind. He asked Essjay to resign from Wikipedia. The Essjay controversy highlighted an important point about Wikipedia: users can never be completely sure who is writing the articles.

STRENGTHS AND WEAKNESSES

As the scandals of 2005 and 2007 indicate, there are weaknesses in Wikipedia. Since the site is not rigorously fact-checked and reviewed like a traditional encyclopedia, it may contain errors and outright falsehoods that have been overlooked. Some articles are better and more complete than others, as the wiki is always growing and changing. The writers and editors of Wikipedia are not necessarily experts, and some articles—especially the newly created ones— are not based on reliable sources. For these reasons, many teachers and professors warn their students not to trust Wikipedia. In 2007, for example, the history department of Middlebury College in Vermont banned the use of Wikipedia as a source for research papers. Many other schools have similar restrictions.

Although Wikipedia is not the most reliable source for research, many teachers would admit that it has strengths. It contains many more articles than any other encyclopedia. The most complete version of *Encyclopædia Britannica* contains approximately 120,000 entries, but English Wikipedia had more than 3 million as of 2010. Wikipedia is constantly being updated so that the latest information is available. It is generally written in a style that is easy to understand and gives a thorough overview of many topics. Best of all, Wikipedia is a collaborative effort—if users see a mistake, they are welcome to fix it.

The safest tactic, then, is to read a Wikipedia article as a starting point for general background about a subject. Check the sources cited in the footnotes to verify any facts and to delve deeper. Wales himself makes no claims that Wikipedia is error-free. He puts it this way: "It is a work in progress and subject to change, but for the most part, people find it reasonably accurate."[5] +

Students in the history department at Middlebury College are not allowed to use Wikipedia for their classes.

Wikipedia is owned by the nonprofit Wikimedia Foundation.

NEW VENTURES

As of 2010, Wikipedia was the largest and most popular encyclopedia in the world. It had more than 15 million articles, more than 3 million of them in English. More than 91,000 active Wikipedians write and edit the encyclopedia every day. Each month, the site attracts more than 68 million visitors, making it one of the top ten most-visited Web sites on the planet.

Since 2003, Wikipedia has been owned by the Wikimedia Foundation, a nonprofit charitable organization. Wikimedia also operates a number of other wiki projects, including Wiktionary (an online dictionary), Wikiquote (an online collection of quotations), and Wikinews (a news wiki). Although most of those working for Wikimedia are volunteers, the foundation uses donations to pay for computer equipment, Web hosting, and some employees.

Wikipedia would likely be worth billions of dollars if it were open to advertisements, but its founders, volunteers, and the Wikimedia Foundation are strongly against using the resource for profit. "Certainly there can be no investment in Wikipedia," Wales said in 2008. "Wikipedia is a nonprofit and always will be."[1]

TOP TEN SITES

The Web site Alexa.com measures Internet traffic and lists the most popular Web sites and pages. In August 2010, Wikipedia was ranked on the list of the top ten most-visited Web sites in the United States:

1. Google.com
2. Facebook.com
3. YouTube.com
4. Yahoo.com
5. Live.com
6. Baidu.com
7. Wikipedia.org
8. Blogger.com
9. MSN.com
10. Tencent.com

JIMMY WALES

Wikipedia's nonprofit status means that Wales will never be paid a salary from the encyclopedia he helped to found. However, with the growth of Wikipedia, Wales's life has changed quite a bit. Today, he is famous—a rock star of the technology scene. He flies all over the world for speaking engagements, promoting Wikipedia and his other business work. He commented in 2007, "I spend 250 days a year around the world . . . . Wikipedia is a global phenomenon. There's a lot of interest in it, and I'm always promoting it, especially in the developing world."[2]

In 2004, Wales and a business partner named Angela Beesley Starling started a for-profit business called Wikia. Wikia is a wiki-farm—a free, wiki-hosting service that allows visitors to create and explore wiki communities. Wikia

WIKIPEDIA SISTER PROJECTS

In addition to Wikipedia, the Wikimedia Foundation runs the following wiki sites:

Wiktionary—A free online dictionary

Wikimedia Commons—A collection of images and sound files

Wikibooks—Educational textbooks that anyone can edit

Wikisource—An online library of free content publications

Wikinews—News stories

Wikiquote—Quotations

Wikispecies—A directory of species

Wikiversity—A learning community where users can find and share educational resources and take online courses

Angela Beesley Starling is cofounder of Wikia.

users have created wikis based on topics from video games and television shows to recipes and crafts. Many of these sites are supported by advertisements that appear on the pages. Wales stepped down as CEO of Wikia in 2006 but still travels around the world to promote the company. In 2008, he introduced a new search site on Wikia called Wikia Search. The site was not as successful as planned, and Wales shut it down a year later. "If there is one thing that I've learned in my career, it is to do more of what's working, and less of what's not."[3]

In 2006, Wales was named one of *Time* magazine's most influential people. He has received many awards for his contributions to the world of electronic learning.

LARRY SANGER AND CITIZENDIUM

After leaving Wikipedia, Sanger began a new encyclopedia called Citizendium. Like Wikipedia, Citizendium is an open-content wiki. Unlike Wikipedia, Citizendium has strict editing rules and requires contributors to reveal their real names and identities. Sanger started Citizendium in the hopes of creating a more reliable online encyclopedia. However, at only approximately 13,000 articles as of 2010, Sanger's project has a long way to go before it can rival Wikipedia. Sanger also started a wiki called WatchKnow, which offers educational videos for teachers and students.

Sanger has said that he believes wikis can be very powerful tools but that they also have their drawbacks and are not good for every type of project. For instance, he is critical of projects such as Wiktionary, the online dictionary, and Wikisource, the online free library, because he believes the collaborative wiki format, with no oversight by experts or editors, makes these resources too unreliable. "The wiki format is not a magic pill that somehow makes all problems go away," he warns.[4]

THE FUTURE OF WIKIPEDIA

In 1962, Charles Van Doren, who would later become the senior editor of *Britannica*, complained that the encyclopedias of his day were lifeless. "The ideal encyclopedia should be radical," he said. "It should stop being safe."[5]

Many Wikipedians have kept Van Doren's ideas in mind while helping to create a new type of encyclopedia. Wikipedia is certainly radical, revolutionary, and alive. It has forever changed the way people find information. And it is growing every day.

The growth of English Wikipedia has begun to slow, however, as editors concentrate more on improving existing articles and less on adding new

WIKIS, WIKIS, EVERYWHERE

Wikipedia is only the most famous of wikis. The World Wide Web has grown to become more interactive and collaborative than ever before. Users can find a wiki for almost anything imaginable—travel, health, music, and more. There are also other wiki encyclopedia projects that aim to be more reliable than Wikipedia. One of them is Scholarpedia.com, an encyclopedia about scientific topics. Some Web sites even provide users with the tools to create their own wikis. Thanks to Wikipedia, wikis are fairly well known today.

JIMMY WALES ON SUCCESS

Speaking at a conference in 2010, Wales offered some ideas on how to be successful as an entrepreneur:

- Fail faster. If a project is doomed, shut it down quickly.
- Don't tie your ego to any one project. If it stumbles, you'll be unable to move forward.
- Real entrepreneurs fail.
- Fail a lot. But enjoy yourself along the way.
- If you handle these things well, "you will succeed."[6]

ones. Still, articles will continue to be added as Wikipedia stays current with the latest topics and world events. Work on Wikipedia will never be truly finished. Internationally, the encyclopedia can expect growth in developing countries, especially in India and throughout Africa, as more people there begin to go online to find and share information. +

Today, Wales travels the world to promote Wikia and Wikipedia.

TIMELINE

1966	1968	1986
Jimmy Donal Wales is born on August 7 in Huntsville, Alabama.	Lawrence Mark Sanger is born on July 16 in Bellevue, Washington.	Sanger graduates from high school and enrolls at Reed College in Portland, Oregon.

1996	1998	2000
Wales and two partners start the Web site Bomis.	Wales quits his financial trading job in Chicago, Illinois, and moves to San Diego, California.	Wales hires Sanger as editor in chief of Nupedia. Sanger moves to San Diego in February.

1989	1991	1995
Wales graduates from Auburn University in Alabama with a bachelor's degree in finance.	Sanger graduates with a bachelor's degree in philosophy. Wales earns a master's degree in finance.	Sanger earns a master's degree in philosophy from Ohio State University.

2000	2000	2001
In June, Sanger completes his PhD in philosophy from Ohio State University.	The first article appears on Nupedia in September.	Wikipedia.com is launched on January 15.

TIMELINE

2001	2002	2003
The first non-English Wikipedias— Spanish, French, and German— appear in March.	In March, Larry Sanger leaves Wikipedia.	In June, Wikipedia becomes a nonprofit site, Wikipedia.org, run by the Wikimedia Foundation.

2006	2007	2007
Wales is named one of the year's most influential people by *Time* magazine.	Sanger launches Citizendium.com.	Sanger launches the site WatchKnow in November.

2004	2004	2005
Wikipedia reaches a total of 1 million articles in more than 100 languages.	Wales and Angela Beesley Starling found the for-profit company Wikia.	A false statement about John Seigenthaler starts a debate about Wikipedia's reliability.

2008	2010	2010
Wales introduces Wikia Search, but abandons it the following year.	English Wikipedia reaches more than 3 million articles.	Wikipedia receives a donation of $2 million from Google.

ESSENTIAL FACTS

CREATORS

Jimmy Wales, August 7, 1966

Larry Sanger, July 16, 1968

DATE LAUNCHED

January 15, 2001

CHALLENGES

Prior to launching Wikipedia, Wales and Sanger attempted to create a carefully reviewed free online encyclopedia called Nupedia, which failed due to its lengthy writing and editing processes. Wikipedia faced issues with users called trolls, who ignited unnecessary controversy on the site. Wikipedia's value as an accurate research tool has also been questioned.

SUCCESSES

Wikipedia grew to become the world's largest and most popular encyclopedia in just a few years. In 2004, it reached 1 million entries, and by 2010 it had more than 15 million. In 2007, Wikipedia became one of the top ten most-visited sites. As of August 2010, it was the seventh most-visited site in the United States.

IMPACT ON SOCIETY

Wikipedia would be worth billions of dollars as a for-profit venture, but the Web site remains a nonprofit. It provides free information on thousands of topics to people all around the world.

QUOTE

"Imagine a world in which every single person on the planet is given free access to the sum of all human knowledge. That's what we're doing." —*Jimmy Wales*

GLOSSARY

blog
> Short for *weblog*; an online journal or diary.

bot
> Also referred to as robot, a computer program designed to perform tasks automatically.

entrepreneur
> A person who creates and manages a new business usually with some risk involved.

hacker
> A skilled computer programmer; may also describe people who illegally break into computer systems.

HTML
> Hypertext markup language, a computer language used to create Web pages and Web sites.

HTTP
> Hypertext transfer protocol, a set of rules for computers to communicate with one another on the Web.

Internet
> A vast worldwide network of computers, all able to communicate using a specific set of rules, or protocols, most importantly TCP/IP.

IP address
> An Internet Protocol address; the unique set of numbers assigned to each computer connected to the Internet. It can sometimes be used to identify a user's geographical location.

libelous
Containing a published untrue and damaging statement about a person.

philosophy
The study of basic ideas about such things as beauty, truth, and knowledge.

sock puppet
A fake identity used for the purpose of tricking others or pretending to be someone else online.

troll
Someone who tries to stir up conflict on the Internet by posting controversial or inappropriate messages.

URL
Universal resource locator; the address of a site on the Web.

username
An identification used by someone accessing an online network.

wiki
A Web site or group of sites that visitors can write and edit themselves using wiki software.

World Wide Web
A collection of hyperlinked documents residing on the Internet that appears as Web pages.

ADDITIONAL RESOURCES

SELECTED BIBLIOGRAPHY

Berners-Lee, Tim. *Weaving the Web: The Original Design and Ultimate Destiny of the World Wide Web.* New York: HarperCollins, 2000. Print.

Lih, Andrew. *The Wikipedia Revolution.* New York: Hyperion, 2009. Print.

Miller, Michael. *Sams Teach Yourself Wikipedia in 10 Minutes.* Indianapolis, IN: Pearson Education, 2010. Print.

FURTHER READINGS

Cindrich, Sharon. *A Smart Girl's Guide to the Internet: How to Connect with Friends, Find What You Need, and Stay Safe Online.* Middleton, WI: American Girl Publishing, 2009. Print.

Hamilton, John. *Internet.* Edina, MN: ABDO Publishing, 2005. Print.

Jakubiak, David. *A Smart Kid's Guide to Doing Internet Research (Kids Online).* New York: PowerKids Press, 2009. Print.

WEB LINKS

To learn more about Wikipedia, visit ABDO Publishing Company online at **www.abdopublishing.com.** Web sites about Wikipedia are featured on our Book Links page. These links are routinely monitored and updated to provide the most current information available.

PLACES TO VISIT

Computer History Museum
1401 N. Shoreline Boulevard, Mountain View, CA 94043
650-810-1010
www.computerhistory.org
Located in the heart of Silicon Valley, California, where computer technology began, the Computer History Museum displays one of the world's largest collections of computer artifacts.

The Tech Museum
201 South Market Street, San Jose, CA 95113
408-294-8324
www.thetech.org
The Tech Museum has hundreds of exhibits focusing on science and technology.

SOURCE NOTES

CHAPTER 1. A NEW KIND OF ENCYCLOPEDIA

1. Larry Sanger. "[Nupedia-L] Let's make a wiki." Message to Nupedia Listserv. 10 Jan. 2001. E-mail.

2. Jimmy Wales. "Forward." *The Wikipedia Revolution.* New York: Hyperion, 2009. Print. xv.

CHAPTER 2. GROWING UP CURIOUS

1. Kelly Kazek. "Wikipedia Founder, Huntsville Native Jimmy Wales, Finds Fame 'Really Cool.'" *The News Courier.* The News-Courier, 12 Aug. 2006. Web. 2 Feb. 2010.

2. Jimmy Wales. "Q & A with Jimmy Wales: Wikipedia Founder." *Q&A.* National Cable Satellite Corporation, 25 Sept. 2005. Web. 2 Feb. 2010.

3. Ibid.

4. Kelly Kazek. "Wikipedia Founder, Huntsville Native Jimmy Wales, Finds Fame 'Really Cool.'" *The News Courier.* The News-Courier, 12 Aug. 2006. Web. 2 Feb. 2010.

5. Ibid.

6. Elisa Lipsky-Karasz. "Mr. Know-It-All." *WMagazine.com.* W Magazine, Sept. 2008. Web. 2 Feb. 2010.

CHAPTER 3. THE INTERNET EXPLOSION

1. Bill Clinton. "Princeton University Commencement Address." *Britannica.com.* Encyclopædia Britannica Online, 4 Jun. 1996. Web. 5 Feb. 2010.

2. Andrew Lih. *The Wikipedia Revolution.* New York: Hyperion, 2009. Print. 26.

3. Larry Sanger. "The Early History of Nupedia and Wikipedia, Part II." *Slashdot.* Geeknet, Inc., 19 Apr. 2005. Web. 2 Feb. 2010.

CHAPTER 4. THE NUPEDIA CONCEPT

1. Larry Sanger. "Nupedia.com Editorial Policy Guidelines (Version 4)." *Nupedia.com.* n.p. May 2000. Web. 13 Feb. 2010.

2. Larry Sanger. "The Early History of Nupedia and Wikipedia: A Memoir." *Slashdot.* Geeknet, Inc., 18 Apr. 2005. Web. 2 Feb. 2010.

3. Ibid.

4. Larry Sanger. "Nupedia.com Editorial Policy Guidelines (Version 4)." *Nupedia.com.* n.p. May 2000. Web. 13 Feb. 2010.

5. Jimmy Wales. "Q & A with Jimmy Wales: Wikipedia Founder." *Q&A.* National Cable Satellite Corporation, 25 Sept. 2005. Web. 2 Feb. 2010.

6. Ibid.

CHAPTER 5. MAKING A WIKI

1. Larry Sanger. "My Role in Wikipedia (links)." *LarrySanger.org.* n.p., n.d. Web 12 Feb. 2010.

2. Larry Sanger. "The Early History of Nupedia and Wikipedia: A Memoir." *Slashdot.* Geeknet, Inc., 18 Apr. 2005. Web. 2 Feb. 2010.

3. Ibid.

4. Jimmy Wales. "Vision: Wikipedia and the Future of Free Culture." *The Long Now Foundation.* The Long Now Foundation, Apr. 2006. Web. 13 Feb. 2010.

5. Larry Sanger. "Wikipedia Is Wide Open. Why Is It Growing So Fast? Why Isn't It Full of Nonsense?" *Kuro5hin.* Kuro5hin Dot Org, 24 Sept. 2001. Web. 13 Feb. 2010.

CHAPTER 6. WIKIPEDIA TAKES OFF

1. Jimmy Wales. "Q & A with Jimmy Wales: Wikipedia Founder." *Q&A.* National Cable Satellite Corporation, 25 Sept. 2005. Web. 2 Feb. 2010.

2. Larry Sanger. "The Early History of Nupedia and Wikipedia, Part II." *Slashdot.* Geeknet, Inc., 19 Apr. 2005. Web. 2 Feb. 2010.

3. Ibid.

4. Jimmy Wales. "Q & A with Jimmy Wales: Wikipedia Founder." *Q&A.* National Cable Satellite Corporation, 25 Sept. 2005. Web. 2 Feb. 2010.

5. Marshall Poe. "The Hive." *The Atlantic.* The Atlantic Monthly Group, Sept. 2006. Web. 2 Feb. 2010.

6. Larry Sanger. "The Early History of Nupedia and Wikipedia: A Memoir." *Slashdot.* Geeknet, Inc., 18 Apr. 2005. Web. 2 Feb. 2010.

SOURCE NOTES CONTINUED

CHAPTER 7. GOING INTERNATIONAL

1. Larry Sanger. "Subject: Announcement about my involvement in Wikipedia and Nupedia." Message posted to list science.linguistics. wikipedia.international. Feb. 2002. Web. 20 Feb. 2010.

2. Edgar Enyedy. "Subject: Good luck with your wikiPAIDia." Message posted to list science.linguistics.wikipedia.international. Feb. 2002. Web. 20 Feb. 2010.

3. Paul Marks. "Interview: Knowledge to the People." *NewScientist.* Reed Business Information Ltd., 31 Jan. 2007. Web. 20 Feb. 2010.

4. Dave Lee. "Wikipedia's Future in Africa." *BBC News.* BBC, 13 Nov. 2009. Web. 20 Feb. 2010.

5. "Wikipedia Editor Larry Sanger Resigns." *Kuro5hin.* Kuro5hin Dot Org, 1 Mar. 2002. Web. 20 Feb. 2010.

CHAPTER 8. TROLLS, VANDALS, AND EDIT WARS

1. "Jimmy Wales." *The Knowledge Trust.* The Knowledge Trust, 2008. Web. 7 Sept. 2010.

2. Larry Sanger. "My Role in Wikipedia (links)." *LarrySanger.org.* n.p., n.d. Web. 12 Feb. 2010.

3. Janet Kornblum. "It's Online, But Is It True?" *USA Today.* USA Today, 6 Dec. 2005. Web. 20 Feb. 2010.

4. Larry Sanger. "The Early History of Nupedia and Wikipedia, Part II." *Slashdot.* Geeknet, Inc., 19 Apr. 2005. Web. 2 Feb. 2010.

5. Larry Sanger. "Is Wikipedia an Experiment in Anarchy?" *Wikimedia.* n.p. 1 Nov. 2001. Web. 2 Feb. 2010.

6. Larry Sanger. "Why Wikipedia Must Jettison Its Anti-Elitism." *Kuro5hin.* Kuro5hin Dot Org, 31 Dec. 2004. Web. 20 Feb. 2010.

CHAPTER 9. CONTROVERSY

1. Larry Sanger. "Quote of the Day." *AskMen.com.* IGN Entertainment, 12 Oct. 2009. Web. 20 Feb. 2010.

2. Brian Chase. "Wikipedia Joker Eats Humble Pie." *BBC News.* BBC, 12 Dec. 2005. Web. 20 Feb. 2010.

3. John Seigenthaler. "A False Wikipedia 'Biography.'" *USA Today.* USA Today, 29 Nov. 2005. Web. 20 Feb. 2010.

4. Stacy Schiff. "Know It All: Can Wikipedia Conquer Expertise?" *The New Yorker.* Condé Nast Digital, 31 Jul. 2006. Web. 20 Feb. 2010.

5. Axel Bruns. *Blogs, Wikipedia, Second Life and Beyond: From Production to Produsage.* New York: Peter Lang Publishing. Print. 147.

CHAPTER 10. NEW VENTURES

1. Noam Cohen. "Open-Source Troubles in Wiki World." *New York Times.* New York Times, 17 Mar, 2008. Web. 20 Feb. 2010.

2. Edward Lewine. "The Encyclopedist's Lair." *New York Times.* New York Times, 18 Nov. 2007. Web. 20 Feb. 2010.

3. Jimmy Wales. Blog post: "Update on Wikia—doing more of what's working." *Jimmy Wales.* n.p. 31 Mar. 2009. Web. 20 Feb. 2010.

4. Larry Sanger. "The Early History of Nupedia and Wikipedia, Part II." *Slashdot.* Geeknet, Inc., 19 Apr. 2005. Web. 2 Feb. 2010.

5. Daniel Pink. "The Book Stops Here." *Wired.* Condé Nast Digital, Mar. 2005. Web. 20 Feb. 2010.

6. Richard Mullins. "Wikipedia Creator Had Lots of Earlier Failures." *TBO.com.* Media General Communications Holdings, 19 Feb. 2010. Web. 20 Feb. 2010.

INDEX

Apple II, 17

ArbCom, 78

Bomis, 8–9, 27, 30, 40, 65, 74

Chalkboard, 56–57

Chase, Brian, 82–83

Chinese Wikipedia, 62, 63

Citizendium, 92

Clinton, Bill, 25

Commodore PET, 17

copyleft, 29, 35

Cunctator, The, 73–74

Cunningham, Ward, 10, 44

Davis, Michael, 8, 27

Diebold, 84

edit wars, 72–73

Encarta, 34

Encyclopædia Britannica, 7, 8, 34, 81, 86

Enyedy, Edgar, 64–66

Essjay, 83–85

exclusionists, 55

GNU, 29, 51

hackers, 27–29

Huntsville, Alabama, 16–17

Ilys, Seth, 52–53

inclusionists, 54–55

Kovitz, Ben, 9

Linux, 29

Manske, Magnus, 44

McHenry, Robert, 81

MediaWiki, 44, 45

Nupedia,
editing process, 37–38
hiring, 31–32
problems, 9, 38–40
volunteers, 9, 35–37

philosophy, 9, 21–22, 30, 31

Rambot, 52, 53

Ramsey, Derek, 52–53

Rand, Ayn, 22

Sanger, Gerry (father), 20–21

Sanger, Larry,
   childhood, 20–21
   education, 20–21, 30
   hired by Nupedia, 31–32
   leaving Wikipedia, 75
   marriage, 74
Seigenthaler, John, 82–83
Shell, Tim, 8, 27, 30
sock puppets, 77–78
Spanish Wikipedia, 64–66
Stallman, Richard, 28–29, 35
Starling, Angela Beesley, 90

Torvalds, Linus, 29
trolls, 71–78, 84

UseMod Wiki, 44

Van Doren, Charles, 93
vandals, 44, 48, 76–78

Wales, Doris (mother), 14–16
Wales, Jimmy,
   childhood, 14–17
   education, 16–17, 19–20
   honors, 92
Wales, Jimmy, Sr. (father), 15

WatchKnow, 92
Wikia, 90–91
Wikia Search, 91
Wikimedia Foundation, 67, 89, 90
Wikipedia,
   administrators, 45, 56
   becoming nonprofit, 66–67
   community, 40, 47–48, 53–54
   deleting entries, 44, 45, 55–56, 72
   reliability, 81, 85–86
WikiWikiWeb, 10, 44
Willy on Wheels, 77
World Book, 7, 14–15, 81

Y2K, 30–31

ABOUT THE AUTHOR

Jennifer Joline Anderson has been writing since she was a teenager, when she won a contest and had her first short story published in *Seventeen* magazine. For most of her career, she has been a writer and editor of literature and language arts textbooks and other educational materials. Today, she lives in Minneapolis, Minnesota, where she writes and edits books for young people.

PHOTO CREDITS